A Gristly Tail

by
CHARLES H. STINSON

STARCHAND PRESS
San Francisco

A Gristly Tail
© Charles H. Stinson 2016

Illustrations, Text & Cover Design: Charles H. Stinson

© Starchand Press
1890 Bryant Street, #300
San Francisco, CA 94110, USA
www.StarchandPress.com

The images were originally created as monotypes using a Wright Press; the impressions were scanned and digitally modified for the book using Adobe Photoshop®. Book design was executed with Adobe InDesign® using Optima font.

ISBN 978-0-9858515-1-4

A Gristly Tail

For as long as he could remember, Bumpass had two big Wowsers, who groomed, fed, patted, and cuddled him. Bumpy, as they called him, was born with a dislocated hip; when the Wowsers adopted him, the Veterinarian proclaimed "Bumpy needs surgery within the month." . . . *That sounds ugly*, thought Bumpy.

Bumpy began his personal physical therapy: He ran up trees and ran down trees and balanced on fences and leaped at birds and bugs and leaves and twigs and shadows and daydreams. Then on the day for his surgery, the Veterinarian pronounced, "His hip is cured: Bumpy no longer needs surgery!"

Glad I didn't need any Shpergeries, said Bumpy.

His Wowsers thought Bumpy was without a doubt the best cat on earth, even in the whole universe (at least that part west of the Lampasas River, if not beyond). He was gorgeously handsome. Everyone exclaimed: "Bumpy should do cat food commercials." Even that bratty sister with the huge, fluffy tail thought so.

B ut Bumpy desired neither fortune nor fame, though he was proud of his exceptional looks and elegant fluffy tail. OK, his tail was skinny; but it was wondrously long and dextrous, not ridiculously huge and fluffy.

Bumpy was more than young king of the jungle; he was The King of All of the Jungles in the Entire Back Yard. And sometimes King of the neighbor's back yard, and even of the little park across the street – if that snarly enormous snaggle-toothed cat was away and no one was walking one of those silly Woofers on leashes. *Too bad they didn't have cats*, thought Bumpy.

Bumpy was smart, too, and famous for laconically quipping epigrammatic responses to questions of trite, tricky trivia:

Q: What says one on stubbing a toe?	A: *"Ow"*
Q: Name a famous Chinese revolutionary.	A: *"Mao"*
Q: What is a synonym for 'fight'?	A: *"Row"*
Q: Name an exclamatory interjection.	A: *"Wow!"*
Q: When would you like to eat?	A: *"Now!"*

All of a sudden, all at once, one day, one time when he was not looking or paying much attention, and without any warning or ever so much whatsoever at all, Bumpy was older and more frail. His busy schedule of nap, hunt, nap, eat, nap, run, nap, pounce and nap became more like nap, nap, nap, eat, nap, nap, nap.

Then Bumpy became sick. The Veterinarian told the Wowsers "Give Bumpy Medicine. Twice a day. With a needle."

Bumpy did not mind and soon felt well enough to play bat-a-string and even to chase his gigantic, huge fluffy tail. OK, ok: His skinny tail.

But then all at once one day Bumpy became really, really sick. He could not walk or eat or clean himself or do anything else by himself — except softly to purr with love as his Wowsers cuddled him, cleaned him, fed him, and cried with him. Even that bratty sister licked his face clean when Bumpy was too tired to go on.

Very soon Bumpy simply could not carry on. His Wowsers carried him to his Favorite Garden where he was King of The Very Biggest Jungle in the Whole Back Yard. There they gave him his most favorite treat: A bowl of juice from a can of tuna fish.

Then the Wowsers held Bumpy to their hearts as the Veterinarian gave him medicine to bring the sleep of endless dreams.

Feels like the very best nap ever, thought Bumpy.

Brief Eternity!

Caress of an instant . . .
Like mercury through open fingers:
Such substance! Then . . .
Nothing.

Gone?

What never was

Has nowhere to go.

I suppose,
if I had fingers,

thought Bumpy,

and whatever mercury is.

His Wowsers dug a deep hole in his most favorite spot in the garden at the base of his most favorite climbing tree, a *Metasequoia glyptostroboides*, known only from fossils and thought extinct until discovered in central China. Bumpy would have wanted you to know this because one of his Wowsers mentioned it often, so clearly it was a Very Important Tree.

His Wowsers wrapped and laid Bumpy to rest in his most comfy blanket, with catnip bag by his chin, Teddy Bear pressed to his breast, and tail curled once roundabout to cozy his nose. The Wowsers cried as they touched him one last time, carefully covered him with leaves and moss and soft, fragrant soil, then placed the marvelous rocks from which he had pounced at birds and bugs and leaves and twigs and shadows and daydreams.

His Wowsers lit incense and placed it in the soft turned soil.

Then each held each other in deep tearful hugs.

*H*mm, Bumpy thought in his most delicious nap, *This is not bad at all. Oops,* he said. *What is this? Worms! I used to tease you!* Bumpy said, *Be gentle.*

We will, said the Worms in their own special way, and they were. *Just doing our duty,* they said, and they did.

This is not bad at all, Bumpy said. *Feels just like when my Wowsers tickled my tummy with their fingers.*

He continued his nap.

*O*oh, thought Bumpy. *Plant roots!*

I used to dig down deep in the dirt in order to play with you.

Now you come to visit me!

Welcome home, Bumpy, said the Plant Roots in their own quiet way.

Deep in the soft warm soil, Bumpy slowly disappears, just like that famous Cheshire cat cousin, so very long, long ago.

And although there is less and less and less of Bumpy in the soil down below, there is more and more of him in his beloved and lovely green garden above. The skinny bones of that wondrous tail still slowly feed his garden, where new kitties climb and leap and play.

Deep in his endless most luxurious nap ever Bumpy dreams. *Ooh,* he thinks, *ooh. So this is how the flowers bloom.*

This book is dedicated to my father, James Cotton Stinson (1922-2007), who through example taught me compassion and respect for critters of all shapes and sizes, macro- to microscopic; and also, of course, to the parade of feline fuzzies that fill our lives with companionship, love and amusement.

www.ingramcontent.com/pod-product-compliance
Lightning Source LLC
Chambersburg PA
CBHW041556040426
42447CB00002B/198